Geology Rocks!

Minerals

Rebecca Faulkner

www.raintreepublishers.co.uk
Visit our website to find out more information about **Raintree** books.

To order:
☎ Phone 44 (0) 1865 888112
🖹 Send a fax to 44 (0) 1865 314091
💻 Visit the Raintree bookshop at **www.raintreepublishers.co.uk** to browse our catalogue and order online.

First published in Great Britain by Raintree,
Halley Court, Jordan Hill, Oxford OX2 8EJ,
part of Harcourt Education.
Raintree is a registered trademark
of Harcourt Education Ltd.

Editorial: Melanie Waldron and Rachel Howells
Design: Victoria Bevan
and AMR Design Ltd (www.amrdesign.com)
Illustrations: David Woodroffe
Picture Research: Melissa Allison and Mica Brancic
Production: Duncan Gilbert

Originated by Chroma Graphics Pte. Ltd
Printed and bound in China by
South China Printing Company

ISBN 978 1406 20651 7

11 10 09 08 07
10 9 8 7 6 5 4 3 2 1

**British Library Cataloguing in
Publication Data**
Faulkner, Rebecca.
  Minerals. – (Geology Rocks!)
  549
A full catalogue record for this book is available
from the British Library.

Acknowledgements
The publishers would like to thank the following for
permission to reproduce photographs:

Alamy p. **14** (Mark Baigent); Corbis p. **24** (Frank
Lane Picture Agency/Maurice Nimmo), p. **23** (Gary
Braasch), p. **28** (Jose Manuel Sanchis Calvete);
GeoScience Features Picture Library p. **9**, pp. **12, 15
bottom, 30 right** (A. Fisher), p. **22** (D. Edwards),
pp. **11, 36** (G. Cook), pp. **5, 8, 10, 17, 33 top
left, 40, 41** (Prof. B. Booth); Getty Images pp. **5
bottom inset, 15 top** (National Geographic/Philip
Schermeister), p. **29 bottom** (The Image Bank/Jeff
Smith), p. **4** (Visuals Unlimited/Ken Lucas); Harcourt
Education Ltd. pp. **6 all, 7 all, 34, 38 all, 39 all,**
(Tudor Photography), p. **27 right** (ISTOCK); Natural
Science Photos pp. **21 bottom, 31, 37** (Martin
Land); NHPA p. **44** (ANT Photo Library); Rex Features
p. **33 bottom right** (M. B. Pictures), pp. **5 middle
inset, 32** (Nils Jorgensen); Science Photo Library
p. **43** (Alfred Pasieka), pp. **19, 21 top, 25, 29 top**
(Dirk Wiersma), p. **18** (G. Brad Lewis), p. **13** (Martin
Land), p. **42** (Pascal Goetgheluck), p. **35** (Photo
Library/Roberto De Gugliemo), pp. **5 top right, 26**
(TEK Image), **27 left** (Tony Camacho), p. **30 left**
(Wayne Scherr), p. **20** (Zephyr).

Cover photograph of salt pans in Italy reproduced
with permission of Getty Images (The Image Bank).

Every effort has been made to contact copyright
holders of any material reproduced in this book.
Any omissions will be rectified in subsequent
printings if notice is given to the publishers.

Disclaimer
All the Internet addresses (URLs) given in this book
were valid at the time of going to press. However,
due to the dynamic nature of the Internet, some
addresses may have changed, or sites may have
changed or ceased to exist since publication. While
the author and publishers regret any inconvenience
this may cause readers, no responsibility for any
such changes can be accepted by either the author
or the publishers.

CONTENTS

Any words appearing in the text in bold, **like this,** are explained in the glossary. You can also look out for them in the word bank at the bottom of each page.

MARVELLOUS MINERALS

What do a sparkling diamond ring, the salt you add to your food, and the dull grey graphite in your pencil have in common? They are all minerals.

Minerals come in all shapes and sizes and are found all over the world. Some minerals can be as large as footballs, while others are so tiny we can only see them under a microscope. Some minerals sparkle while others are dull. Some minerals, such as fluorite, glow in the dark. You can even use some minerals as magnets. Some minerals are so hard that they can scratch steel. Other minerals are so soft that they feel powdery and can be scratched easily by your fingernail.

Hard and soft

Diamond is the hardest mineral on Earth so it cannot be scratched by anything else. Graphite is a very soft mineral. If you rub your fingers on a piece of graphite they will be dirty. Graphite is so soft it rubs off on to your fingers.

The mineral smithsonite is found in zinc ore deposits. It can be white, grey, yellow, green, blue, pink, or brown!

All rocks are made of minerals. There are more than 4,000 minerals on Earth, and scientists are still discovering new ones. Most of these 4,000 minerals are very rare.

We can see minerals all around us – in mountain ranges, on the beach, in river beds, and in cliffs. Some minerals can take on amazing forms, while others form beautiful gemstones such as diamonds and rubies.

These mineral formations are called travertine and they form as the water in these hot springs **evaporates**.

Find out later...

How are minerals used in computers?

Why are diamonds so expensive?

Which mineral makes **stalactites**?

stalactite thin icicle-shaped lump of rock that forms as water drips from cave ceilings

WHAT ARE MINERALS?

Minerals are the building blocks of rocks. They occur naturally and are solid substances made up from one or more chemical **elements**. An element is a substance made of tiny particles called **atoms**. There are more than 110 known chemical elements and these can combine together in many different ways to form all the minerals found on Earth.

Minerals usually form shapes, called **crystals**, depending on the elements they contain. The atoms in crystals are arranged in three-dimensional patterns called **lattices**. These have regular geometric shapes such as hexagons or pyramids.

Eight elements

Most of the minerals found on Earth are made up of the following eight elements:

- oxygen
- silicon
- aluminium
- iron
- calcium
- sodium
- potassium
- magnesium.

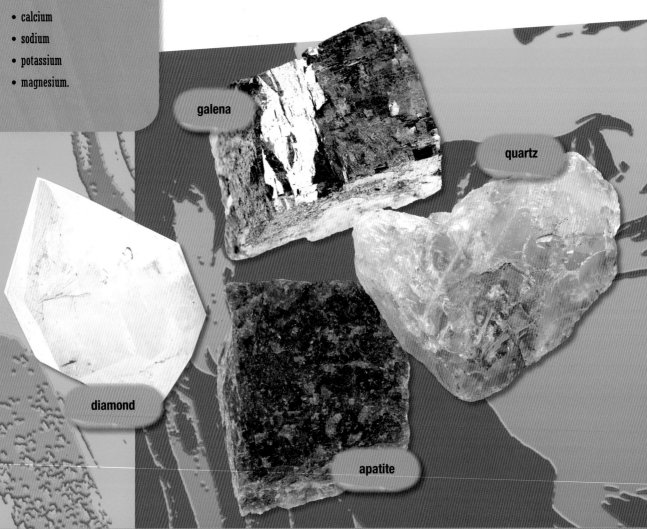

galena

quartz

diamond

apatite

atom tiny particle that elements and minerals are made from
composition what something is made from

Each mineral has an exact chemical **composition** and an exact structure. If you are lucky enough to find a diamond, for example, it will always be made from the element carbon. Its atoms will always be arranged in the same way. Quartz will always contain silicon and oxygen, and the atoms will always be arranged in the same way.

Most minerals are **compounds** made of many elements. The mineral gypsum is made from the elements calcium, oxygen, and sulphur. Only occasionally are minerals made from only one element. The mineral gold contains only the element gold.

Crystals

The word "crystal" comes from the Greek word *krystallos*, which means "ice". The Greeks found beautiful quartz crystals in the Alps and believed that they were a form of water frozen so hard that they would never thaw.

⬇ Minerals come in a variety of shapes, sizes, and colours.

chrome diopside

topaz

hornblende

orthoclase feldspar

compound mixture of elements
element natural substance made up of atoms

7

ROCKY MINERALS

Hard minerals

If a rock contains hard minerals, such as quartz, it will be a hard rock. **Granite** contains lots of quartz, so we know that it is hard.

Different types of mineral combine to make rocks in the same way that ingredients combine to make a salad. You can make a salad that contains a variety of ingredients, such as lettuce, spring onions, and peppers, or you can make a salad that consists only of lettuce. In the same way a rock may contain many different minerals, while another rock may be made up of just one mineral.

The rock-forming minerals

Although there are more than 4,000 minerals on Earth, only about 30 of them usually form rocks. These are called rock-forming minerals. We can **classify** them into groups according to similarities they have with one another. This is called classification. There are eight major mineral groups: native elements, silicates, oxides, sulphides, sulphates, halides, carbonates, and phosphates.

You can see the minerals in this granite. It is made up of the minerals quartz, feldspar, and mica.

Native elements

Most minerals are made up of a mixture of **elements**, but a few minerals occur naturally by themselves as single elements. These are called **native elements**.

Most native elements are metals, such as gold, silver, copper, and platinum, and these are found as nuggets or flakes in rocks. Gold is found glittering in cracks or on the surface of rocks. Lumps of gold can also be found in rocks or in rivers if it has been eroded from the rocks.

Some non-metal minerals, such as diamond, graphite, and sulphur, are also native elements. Diamond is formed deep inside Earth's **crust** at very high temperatures and pressure, whereas graphite is formed at much shallower depths. Bright yellow sulphur is often found near hot springs and volcanoes.

Gold nugget

The largest nugget of gold ever found weighed 71 kilograms (157 pounds). It was found in 1869 in a place called Moliagol in Australia. Large nuggets such as this are extremely rare.

⬆ Only a few minerals are native elements. One of these is sulphur. At these hot springs in Iceland, sulphur is left behind when hot water escapes from deep inside the Earth's crust.

Silicates

Silicates are the most common rock-forming minerals on Earth. Examples include quartz, feldspar, mica, olivine, and pyroxene. There are more than 1,000 different silicate minerals, and they all contain the **elements** silica and oxygen.

The silicates quartz and feldspar are very common and make up the bulk of most rocks. Mica minerals, such as muscovite and biotite, are found in all types of rock and form thin sheets. Quartz is a very tough mineral which is resistant to **weathering**.

Olivine is dark green in colour and can be found on some beaches in volcanic areas such as in Hawaii. Pyroxene is also dark green and is a very common mineral found in most rocks.

Other silicates are very rare, for example garnet, tourmaline, and topaz. These minerals can be found in many different colours.

Tourmaline minerals have vivid colours. Long **crystals** sometimes show two or more colours along their length.

impurity invading substance that enters another substance when it is growing

Oxides

Oxides, such as hematite and magnetite, are made up of a metal combined with oxygen. They usually form deep inside Earth's **crust**. This is another large group of minerals, and oxides are found in all rock types.

Hematite and magnetite contain iron, and have been mined since ancient times. The word "hematite" comes from the Greek word for blood because when it is ground to a powder it is a blood-red colour.

Gemstones such as rubies and sapphires are also oxide minerals. Rubies and sapphires are forms of corundum, which is one of the hardest minerals. The blue colour of sapphires and the red colour of rubies are caused by **impurities** in the minerals. Impurities of chromium form rubies, and impurities of titanium and iron form sapphires.

Magnetic sand

If you see black sand grains on a beach they are likely to be made of the oxide mineral magnetite. If you find a beach that has black sand, try running a magnet over the surface and see whether the little black sand grains stick to it.

The dark mineral magnetite is an important source of iron and is naturally magnetic.

Sulphides

Sulphide minerals such as pyrite, galena, cinnabar, and chalcopyrite are combinations of sulphur and metals. They are often important sources of metals, and many of the minerals in this group look like metals.

Chalcopyrite is a common mineral and is the main source of copper. Galena is made of sulphur and lead and is an important source of lead. Crystals of galena and pyrite form almost perfect cubes. Cinnabar is often found near hot springs in volcanic areas because it forms when hot water **evaporates**. It is bright red in colour and often contains a lot of mercury.

Pyrite and chalcopyrite

Pyrite and chalcopyrite both have a shiny gold metallic colour. Pyrite means fire, and the mineral pyrite gives off sparks when it is struck sharply.

⇨ Pyrite is one of the most widely distributed sulphide minerals. It is found in all types of rock.

Sulphates

Sulphate minerals such as gypsum, anhydrite, and epsomite all contain sulphur and oxygen. There are more than 200 sulphate minerals, but most are rare. They usually form when water evaporates in desert areas or hot water evaporates in volcanic areas – leaving behind mineral deposits. All sulphates are soft and pale coloured. Gypsum is the most common sulphate and has many forms.

Flower-shaped gypsum

Desert rose gypsum forms when water evaporates in hot deserts, and is common in Namibia. It has petal-shaped crystals that look like roses. When water evaporates from hollows on rock surfaces another type of gypsum can form called daisy gypsum. This is so called because it looks like a daisy.

Gypsum is the most common sulphate mineral. It is made from calcium, sulphur, oxygen, and hydrogen.

Halides

You are probably very familiar with the salt you add to your food, but do you know it is a mineral called halite? Halite and fluorite are types of minerals called halides. They are usually soft minerals that dissolve easily in water.

Halite is a very common mineral and can be found in many places around the world. It forms cube-shaped **crystals** as water **evaporates** in desert areas, for example around Salt Lake in Utah, USA. Halite can also be found buried in rocks where ancient oceans have evaporated.

Carbonates and phosphates

The last two groups are carbonates and phosphates. All carbonate minerals, such as calcite, malachite, and azurite, contain carbon and oxygen. Phosphate minerals, such as apatite and turquoise, contain phosphate. Many carbonates and phosphates form at Earth's surface when other minerals are affected by the action of wind and rain.

The salt you add to your food is a mineral called halite. The word "halite" comes from the Greek word meaning salt.

fluorescent substance that glows in ultraviolet light

There are many different types of calcite. Some types form in areas of limestone rocks. Water passing through the rocks picks up calcium carbonate. When this mineral-rich water drips into caves it can form spectacular deposits of calcite that look like icicles. These are called **stalactites** (which hang from the ceiling) and **stalagmites** (which grow up from the floor). The longest stalactite in the world is thought to be in a limestone cave in County Clare, Ireland. It is more than 6 metres (20 feet) long.

Iceland spar

The largest calcite crystal in the world was found in Helgustadir in Iceland. It was a type of calcite called Iceland spar and it measured 7 metres (23 feet) long, 7 metres (23 feet) high, and 2 metres (7 feet) deep. It weighed more than 250,000 kilograms (550,000 pounds).

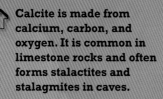

⬆ Calcite is made from calcium, carbon, and oxygen. It is common in limestone rocks and often forms stalactites and stalagmites in caves.

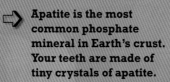

➡ Apatite is the most common phosphate mineral in Earth's crust. Your teeth are made of tiny crystals of apatite.

stalagmite   short, stubby column of rock that forms when water drips
               on to a cave floor and evaporates

MINERAL CREATION

Most minerals form deep inside Earth when hot liquid material cools and hardens to form rock. If we could dig deep into Earth we would see that the inside is made up of different layers.

The **crust** is like a skin around Earth. It is a relatively thin layer covering the surface of Earth. There are two types of crust – continental and oceanic. Continental crust is found beneath the continents and can be up to 70 kilometres (45 miles) thick. Oceanic crust is found beneath the oceans and is about 10 kilometres (6 miles) thick.

Rocky crust

The rocks of Earth's crust are made from minerals. Silicate minerals make up over 90 per cent of the rocks of Earth's crust. We cannot always see these rocks because they may be covered with water, soil, or buildings, but they are definitely there.

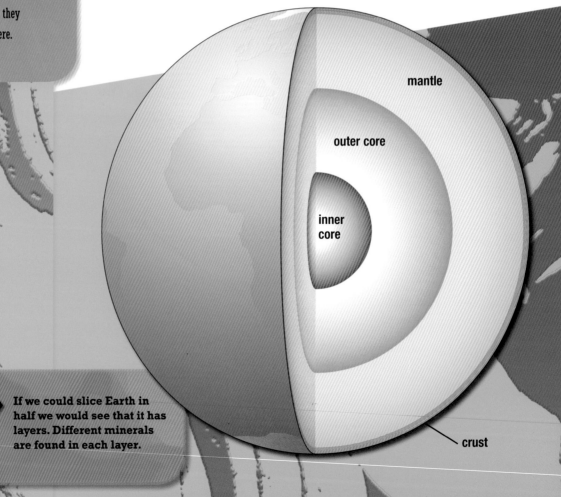

mantle

outer core

inner core

crust

⇨ If we could slice Earth in half we would see that it has layers. Different minerals are found in each layer.

core central layer of Earth
mantle hot layer of Earth beneath the crust

If we could peel away the crust we would find the **mantle**. This is a thick layer that starts at the base of the crust and extends 2,900 kilometres (1,800 miles) deep into Earth. This is where hot liquid material **solidifies** to form minerals.

If you could travel deep down into the centre of Earth you would find the **core**. Here it is even hotter than the mantle. The core is made up of an inner and outer core. The inner core is solid, and the outer core is liquid. Metal minerals are common in the core. Most of the iron on Earth has sunk into the core because it is heavy.

Minerals in the mantle

The rocks in the mantle are so hot – up to 3,000° Celsius (5,500° Fahrenheit) – that they are partly **molten**. Most of the upper mantle is made of olivine minerals because these can form at such high temperatures. Olivine is much more rare in the crust.

⬆ The rocks of Earth's crust are made up of many different types of minerals.

molten melted
solidify become solid

How are minerals formed?

Earth's **crust** is made up of three types of rock:

- igneous rocks
- sedimentary rocks
- metamorphic rocks.

The minerals that create these rocks form in different ways.

Igneous minerals

Minerals are formed in igneous rocks from hot liquid material called **magma** that is found in the **mantle**. Over millions of years the magma rises up from the mantle and travels towards the surface of Earth. As it does so, it cools and hardens to form silicate minerals and native elements, either under ground or at Earth's surface – both on land and under water.

Granite

Granite is an example of a coarse grained igneous rock. It contains the minerals quartz, feldspar, mica, and hornblende. Pegmatite has even coarser grains and may contain the minerals aquamarine, tourmaline, beryl, topaz, cassiterite, fluorite, apatite, tin, and tungsten.

Lava from volcanoes **solidifies** to form igneous rocks.

crystallization cooling and hardening of magma to form igneous rock
lava name for magma when it reaches the surface of Earth

The process of magma cooling and hardening to form minerals is called **crystallization**. If magma cools slowly under ground there is plenty of time for large **crystals** to form, and so the minerals will be large. We say that the rock produced is **coarse grained**.

When magma rises all the way to Earth's surface it is called **lava**. Sometimes this lava erupts on to the surface of the crust through volcanoes. Once on the surface, the lava cools quickly so there is little time for crystals to develop before the rock hardens. As a result of this the minerals will be small, so we say the rock is **fine grained**. **Basalt** is an example of a fine grained igneous rock. It contains the minerals plagioclase and pyroxene.

Feldspar

Granite forms from cooling magma. As the magma cools underground feldspar begins to crystallize first. For this reason feldspar crystals are often larger than crystals of the other minerals. Feldspar is often pink in colour, so granite that contains a lot of it will have a pink appearance.

This granite contains a lot of feldspar, and so has a pinkish colour. It has been eroded by waves for thousands of years to form this unusual shape.

Sedimentary minerals

Some **sedimentary rocks** are formed from broken bits of other rocks. When **igneous rocks** are attacked by wind and rain at Earth's surface tiny particles of rock and minerals are broken off and carried away. These minerals are eventually dropped in a new place. This is called **deposition**. They build up over millions of years to form new sedimentary rock.

Sedimentary rocks can also form when minerals are deposited by water **evaporating** in volcanic areas or from lagoons, seas, and lakes in desert areas. Sulphate and halide minerals, such as gypsum and halite, are formed in this way.

Travertine

Travertine is a calcite-rich rock that forms as water evaporates around hot springs. It often forms **stalactites** and **stalagmites**.

⬆ **This is Champagne Pool in New Zealand. The water contains lots of minerals, including arsenic, mercury, silver, and gold.**

Metamorphic minerals

Metamorphic rocks are formed when heat or high pressure changes igneous or sedimentary rocks. When hot magma rises below Earth's surface it heats up the surrounding rocks. When mountain ranges form on Earth the rocks buried below experience immense pressures. All this extra heat and pressure causes the minerals in the rocks to change (metamorphose) into other minerals. Kyanite and chlorite are examples of metamorphic minerals.

Sulphide minerals

If hot, mineral-rich water comes into contact with rocks it can change them into metamorphic rocks. This process produces sulphide minerals such as pyrite and galena.

Intense heat and pressure can squash the minerals in rocks to create new ones. This metamorphic rock is called gneiss.

Kyanite is a mineral commonly found in metamorphic rocks.

CRYSTALS IN CAVITIES

The rocks of Earth's **crust** are made up of common minerals, but amazing formations of rare minerals are more difficult to find.

Where can we find rare minerals?

Minerals can be found in **igneous, sedimentary,** and **metamorphic rocks,** but the best places to find amazing **crystals** of rare minerals are in cracks and cavities in rocks where the crystals are able to grow freely.

Mineral veins

Rare minerals and large crystals can often be found in **mineral veins.** These are like sheets of minerals that grow in cracks cutting through rocks.

Finding crystals

You can find large crystals of minerals such as quartz, galena, and calcite in mineral veins. If you are lucky you can also find beautiful crystals of very rare minerals such as carnelian.

⬆ Carnelian is a rare mineral that can be found in mineral veins.

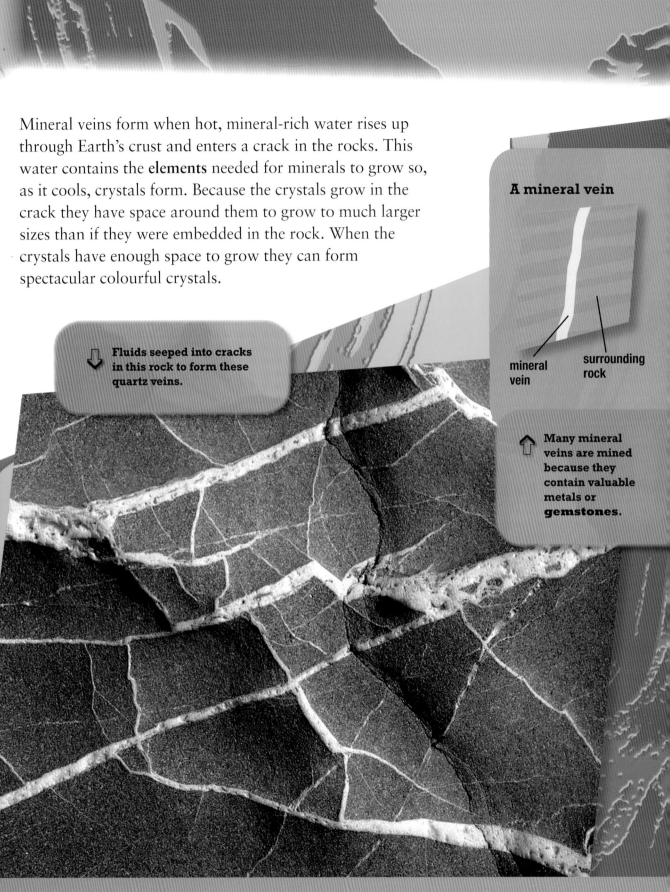

Mineral veins form when hot, mineral-rich water rises up through Earth's crust and enters a crack in the rocks. This water contains the **elements** needed for minerals to grow so, as it cools, crystals form. Because the crystals grow in the crack they have space around them to grow to much larger sizes than if they were embedded in the rock. When the crystals have enough space to grow they can form spectacular colourful crystals.

A mineral vein

mineral vein

surrounding rock

Fluids seeped into cracks in this rock to form these quartz veins.

Many mineral veins are mined because they contain valuable metals or **gemstones**.

Geodes

Amazing formations of minerals can also be found in **geodes**. A geode looks like a normal rock, but when it is split open a lining of beautiful **crystals** is revealed.

A geode usually forms in volcanic areas when **lava** cools. Lava often contains lots of gas bubbles. Sometimes a gas bubble will become trapped as the lava **solidifies** into **igneous rock**. This forms a cavity in the rock, which is an ideal site for minerals to form. When water passes through the lava it will dissolve some of the minerals. This mineral-rich water may become trapped in a cavity, and deposit its minerals there. As the lava cools, the minerals **crystallize** inside the cavity. As there is space around them, the crystals can grow freely to produce spectacular mineral formations.

Geode facts

The most common mineral found in geodes is quartz, in various colourful forms, especially amethyst and agate. Calcite can also be found. The largest geodes are big enough for you to crawl inside.

The cavity inside this geode is the perfect environment for crystal growth. Many geodes like this one are found in Brazil, India, and Russia.

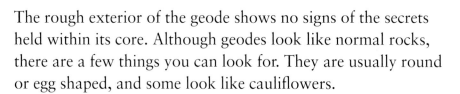

The rough exterior of the geode shows no signs of the secrets held within its core. Although geodes look like normal rocks, there are a few things you can look for. They are usually round or egg shaped, and some look like cauliflowers.

The crystal lining of a geode is revealed only when the rock is split open. One way to open a geode is to put it in a sock and then hit it with a hammer. The sock will stop sharp bits of rock from hitting anyone.

Geodes and nodules

A geode that is completely filled with small, compact crystal formations, such as agate, is called a nodule. The only difference between a geode and a nodule is that a geode has a hollow cavity, whereas a nodule is solid.

Agate forms concentric bands like the rings of a tree trunk. The bands sometimes look like eyes or like landscapes.

HOW IMPORTANT ARE MINERALS?

Minerals are very important in our daily lives. Most of the things you use every day are made from minerals. Your watch, your computer, and even your toothpaste all have parts made from minerals.

Uses of minerals

Some minerals contain metals that can be **extracted** and used for many things from spacecraft, to aeroplanes, to cars, to tin cans. Some minerals are very rare and also very beautiful. These have a huge economic value, and include the precious metals gold and silver, and **gemstones** such as diamonds, sapphires, and rubies.

Quartz is used in making watches because it has a natural electrical charge that keeps time. When an electric current is passed through a quartz crystal it will vibrate at a specific frequency. This means that it will vibrate a certain number of times every second. It is this vibration of the crystal that keeps time in a watch.

Did you know?
You may know that fluoride is added to toothpaste to strengthen our teeth, but did you know that fluorides come from the halide mineral fluorite? Another halide mineral is halite (rock salt), which is used to preserve and flavour our food.

A silicon chip that powers a computer is made from quartz and is about the same size as a fingernail.

The silica in quartz is used to make glass windowpanes, lenses for glasses, and silicon chips. Silicon chips are used in many electronic items from space shuttles, to coffee makers, to traffic lights, to computers.

The colourful nature of some minerals means that they are ground to make **pigments** that are used in paint. The minerals hematite and realgar produce red pigment; limonite and orpiment produce yellow pigment; and azurite produces blue pigment. Cave paintings thousands of years old have been found that use mineral pigments.

The soft mineral talc has many uses. It is so soft it is used to make baby powder and talcum powder. It is also used to make crayons, paint, make-up, paper, and soap. Kaolin is another soft mineral. It is used to make china plates and cups, and is also known as china clay.

Sulphur is mined from under ground and is used to make sulphuric acid. This has many uses in industry. It is used to make fertilizers, paper, paint, and cellophane, for example.

Models use minerals to look good. The soft mineral talc is used to produce make-up.

Halite is mined and piled up in huge salt mountains where it is left to dry out. You can then add it to your food.

Metals from minerals

Magnitogorsk

There is a city in Russia called Magnitogorsk after the unusually high quantities of magnetite found in the mountains surrounding the city. Magnitogorsk is a leading iron manufacturing centre in Russia today.

Some sulphide and oxide minerals are rich in metallic **elements** such as copper and iron. These are called **metal ores** and the metals they produce have many uses. Chalcopyrite is the main ore for copper, which is used for water pipes and electrical wires. Hematite and magnetite are important sources of iron. Iron is used to make steel, which is used to make cars, buses, trains, aeroplanes, and ships.

Once the metal ore has been **extracted** from the ground, by mining or quarrying, it then has to be heated at very high temperatures to separate the metal from the ore. This is called **smelting**.

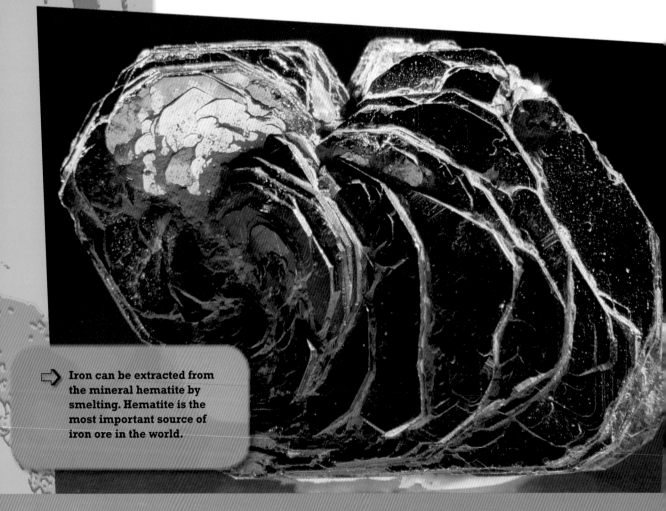

⇨ **Iron can be extracted from the mineral hematite by smelting. Hematite is the most important source of iron ore in the world.**

Some metals do not have to be separated from ores because they are found in rocks as **native elements**. Gold and silver are found in this way and are easy to extract, so have been used by humans for thousands of years. Today gold is mined in open cast mines (large pits in the ground) as well as underground mines. It is estimated that around 2,500 tonnes (2,460 tons) of gold are mined each year – mainly in South Africa, Australia, Russia, and the United States.

Gold is used for jewellery because it never tarnishes and it lasts forever. Because it does not tarnish it is sometimes used by dentists, to make fillings and false teeth. Silver is used for jewellery and cutlery. Gold, silver, and copper are good conductors of electricity. This means they can be used for making wires.

Fool's gold

Gold is a precious metal and is very expensive. Other minerals, such as pyrite and chalcopyrite, look like gold and can be mistaken for it. They therefore have the nickname "fool's gold".

Gold is found as lumps called nuggets in many types of rock. It is extracted from the rock by mining and has many uses.

Copper wires are used in many electronic devices, from mobile phones to computers.

Decorative minerals

Gemstone qualities

A gemstone has three qualities that separate it from other minerals: rarity, beauty, and durability. Rarity and beauty increase its value. Durability (hardness) ensures the gemstone will last for a long time.

Many minerals such as rubies, garnet, emerald, and opal are used in jewellery. Large, richly coloured crystals can occasionally form, and these are worth a lot of money. The different colours are caused by **impurities** in the minerals. The stones are cut and polished in special ways so that light reflects off the surface and the stone sparkles. These are called **gemstones**.

The most valuable gemstones – the precious gemstones – are those that are the rarest, hardest, and most beautiful. They include diamonds, rubies, emeralds, and sapphires.

Other gemstones are called semi-precious gemstones and these are not so expensive. They include garnet, opal, tourmaline, amethyst, and topaz. Garnets form deep inside Earth in **metamorphic rocks** and can be blood-red in colour. Tourmaline, topaz, and amethyst can be found in a huge variety of colours. Colourless topaz is often mistaken for diamond.

⬇ This tourmaline is known as watermelon tourmaline because the colours are the same as a watermelon.

⬆ This sapphire has been carefully cut and polished to bring out the natural beauty of the mineral.

Because precious gemstones are so rare and expensive scientists have learned how to make gemstones artificially. For example, synthetic diamonds can be made from the mineral zirconium. Some of these synthetic gemstones are made so well that it is very difficult to tell they are not real.

Other minerals are used for decoration as well as gemstones. Jade and agates are used for ornaments, statues, vases, and bowls. Agate is one of the most popular minerals for ornamental work because of its striking coloured bands. Jade can be white, colourless, red, or green. It has been used to make jewellery, ornaments, and statues for thousands of years – particularly in China.

Powerful gemstones?

Some gemstones are believed by some to have special powers. The ancient Egyptians made amulets (necklaces) encrusted with gemstones to protect them from harm. The ancient Chinese believed that jade would protect their bodies from decay so they could live forever.

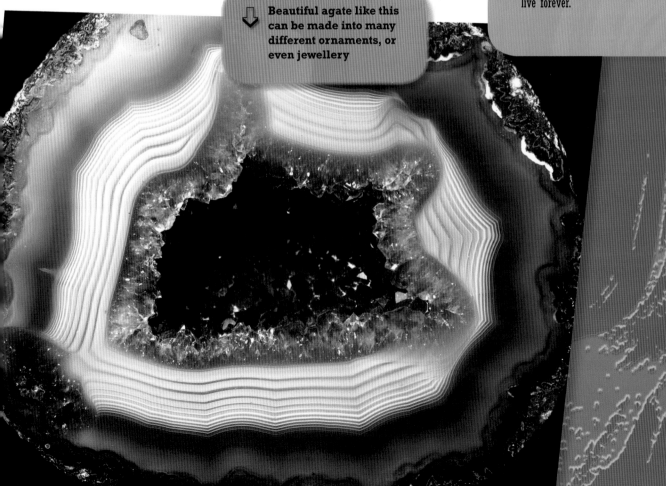

⇩ Beautiful agate like this can be made into many different ornaments, or even jewellery

Gems from the deep

Diamonds are the most valuable of all **gemstones**. They are very rare, and diamond is the hardest known mineral. Diamond is also the most **transparent** mineral known. This means light can pass through it, and this is what makes a diamond sparkle so brightly. Most diamonds are colourless, but **impurities** can make them any colour of the rainbow.

Diamonds form deep in Earth's **mantle** and are subjected to intense pressure and heat, so it is no wonder they are so hard. Over millions of years they are carried to the surface of Earth in **igneous rock** called kimberlite.

Only about 20 per cent of all diamonds found are gemstone quality and can be used in jewellery. Scientists classify diamonds according to the "Four Cs" of carat, clarity, cut, and colour.

Ancient diamonds

Most of the diamonds found on Earth today are older than the dinosaurs – they are billions of years old. Australia produces most of the world's diamonds, but they are also found in South Africa, Brazil, and India.

⬇ This is the world's largest uncut diamond. It weighs 616 carat. Most diamonds you see in engagement rings are less than 1 carat.

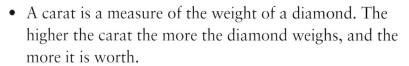

- A carat is a measure of the weight of a diamond. The higher the carat the more the diamond weighs, and the more it is worth.

- Clarity is how clear something is. It is very rare to find a perfectly clear diamond because most contain tiny amounts of impurities that you can only see under a microscope. Diamonds with smaller and less visible impurities have more value.

- The cut is the way the diamond is shaped by skilled diamond polishers. Diamonds are cut in special ways so that light enters and is reflected off different faces to make it sparkle. A diamond has to be cut very carefully because a poor cut will reduce the quality and value.

- Most diamonds have tiny amounts of colour – even though they look colourless. A totally colourless diamond is very rare and expensive.

Diamonds in tools

Most of the diamonds found are too small or shaped too strangely to be used in jewellery. Because diamonds are so hard they are also used in cutting tools and drills. The drill a dentist uses to drill teeth is made of diamond.

⬆ Because diamond is the hardest substance known it makes a useful cutting tool.

➡ Diamonds are a favourite for items of jewellery because of the way they reflect light and sparkle.

HOW CAN WE IDENTIFY MINERALS?

Just as you can see the individual ingredients in a salad you can also identify the individual minerals in a rock. Because there are so many different minerals you may think it is impossible to identify all of them. In order to identify a mineral we need to look at its **properties**. A property is a characteristic of a mineral. These properties include:

- colour
- **streak** (its colour when powdered)
- shape
- hardness
- **density** (how heavy it is)
- **cleavage** (how it breaks)
- **lustre** (how shiny it is).

Colour

When you look at a mineral you will usually notice its colour first. Some minerals are easy to identify by their colour because they are always the same colour. For example, malachite is always green, and azurite is always blue.

⇨ You can be a mineralogist. If you look closely at the rocks you find in your local area you may be able to see what minerals they contain.

Other minerals can vary in colour so it can be difficult to tell what the mineral is just by looking at it. The variations in mineral colours are due to **impurities**.

Pure quartz is called rock crystal and is colourless. Sometimes tiny amounts of impurities, such as iron and aluminium, can enter the **crystal lattice**. When this happens different coloured quartz will be produced:

- purple amethyst can form when impurities of iron are present
- black or brown smoky quartz can form when impurities of aluminium are present
- white milky quartz is the most common type of quartz and forms when small cavities in the quartz are filled with liquids that make it look white
- pink rose quartz can form where impurities of titanium are present.

Colourful minerals
The mineral apatite can be yellow, green, brown, red, purple, or white. Topaz can be colourless, yellow, blue, pink, or orange. Fluorite can be clear, white, yellow, blue, purple, or green.

The mineral topaz can be found in many colours. Clear crystals are used as **gemstones**.

Streak

The **streak** of a mineral is its colour when powdered. You can find out what colour the streak of a mineral is by scraping the mineral along a streak plate. A streak plate is an unglazed, white porcelain tile. When the mineral is rubbed across the streak plate some of the mineral is broken off and ground into a powder.

You may get some surprising results because a mineral's streak colour may be very different from the colour of the mineral **crystals**. The colour of the streak for a particular mineral is always the same. For example, it does not matter whether quartz is purple, white, black, or pink – it always leaves a white streak.

This spiky mineral is called millerite. Its crystals are acicular.

Shape

The shape of individual crystals in a mineral cannot often be seen, but when they can be seen these shapes may help us to identify minerals. Crystals of pyrite and galena often form cubes. Crystals of quartz, beryl, and graphite often form hexagons.

Crystals that have a thread-like appearance are called fibrous. Asbestos is an example of a fibrous mineral. Crystals that have a needle-like appearance, such as those found in the mineral reibeckite, are called acicular. Malachite often occurs in mammilated or botryoidal forms. In mammilated minerals the crystals appear as rounded lumps, and in botryoidal forms they look like a bunch of grapes. If the mineral shows no clear shape we say it is massive.

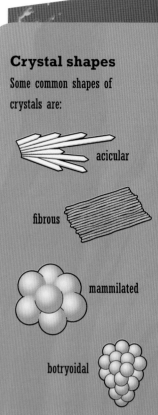

Crystal shapes

Some common shapes of crystals are:

acicular

fibrous

mammilated

botryoidal

⇨ This is a mineral called malachite, showing its botryoidal form.

Hardness

The hardness of a mineral is a measure of its resistance to scratching. Some minerals are very hard. Diamond is the hardest mineral we know about, and it can scratch any other substance. Talc is so soft that you can break it with your fingers.

A German mineralogist called Friedrich Mohs devised a scale of hardness called Mohs' scale of hardness to help with the identification of minerals. In this scale, talc (the softest mineral) has a hardness of 1, and diamond (the hardest mineral) has a hardness of 10. All minerals fall somewhere along the scale between these two extremes.

The minerals with low hardness numbers are soft and easy to scratch. Those with a hardness below 3 are so soft you can scratch them with your fingernail. Minerals with higher hardness numbers are more difficult to scratch. A sharp knife will scratch minerals up to a hardness of 6. The only thing that will scratch a diamond is another diamond.

Writing with rocks

We use chalk to write on a chalkboard because it leaves a mark. Chalk is made from the mineral calcite, and it leaves a mark because it is softer than the chalkboard.

⬇ Mohs' scale of hardness.

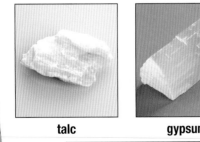

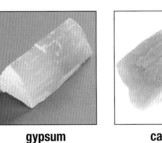

talc	gypsum	calcite	fluorite	apatite
1	2	3	4	5

The hardness of minerals can determine the hardness of the rock that contains them. If a rock contains hard minerals, such as quartz, it will be a hard rock. The rocks **granite** and quartzite contain lots of quartz, so we know that they are hard rocks.

Density

The **density** of a mineral is a measure of how heavy it is for the volume it occupies. Some mineral samples will feel heavier than others – even if all your samples are the same size. The heavier ones have a greater density than the lighter ones.

Scientists can sometimes identify minerals by working out their densities. Metallic minerals, such as platinum, usually have higher densities than non-metallic minerals such as sulphur. Gold is one of the most dense minerals in the world.

Mineral densities

Density	Mineral example
low density	sulphur, graphite
medium density	quartz, gypsum
high density	apatite, fluorite
very high density	galena, pyrite
extremely high density	silver, gold

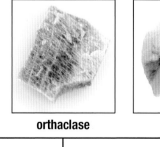

orthaclase

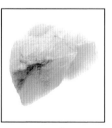

quartz

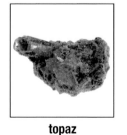

topaz

corundum

diamond

6   7   8   9   10

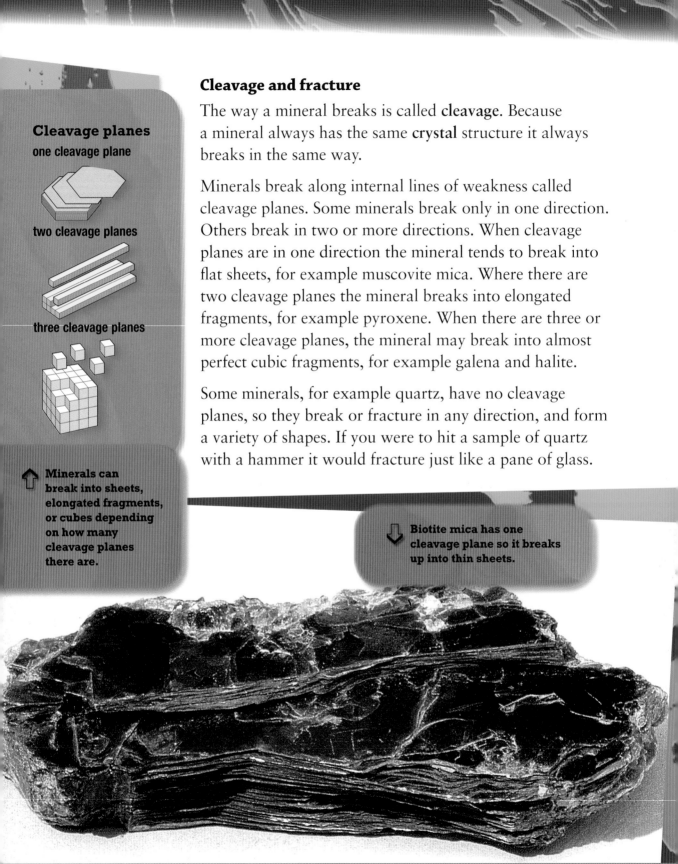

Cleavage planes

one cleavage plane

two cleavage planes

three cleavage planes

⬆ Minerals can break into sheets, elongated fragments, or cubes depending on how many cleavage planes there are.

Cleavage and fracture

The way a mineral breaks is called **cleavage**. Because a mineral always has the same **crystal** structure it always breaks in the same way.

Minerals break along internal lines of weakness called cleavage planes. Some minerals break only in one direction. Others break in two or more directions. When cleavage planes are in one direction the mineral tends to break into flat sheets, for example muscovite mica. Where there are two cleavage planes the mineral breaks into elongated fragments, for example pyroxene. When there are three or more cleavage planes, the mineral may break into almost perfect cubic fragments, for example galena and halite.

Some minerals, for example quartz, have no cleavage planes, so they break or fracture in any direction, and form a variety of shapes. If you were to hit a sample of quartz with a hammer it would fracture just like a pane of glass.

⬇ Biotite mica has one cleavage plane so it breaks up into thin sheets.

Lustre

The **lustre** of a mineral is a measure of its shininess. Some minerals glint and sparkle, whereas others hardly reflect any light at all.

Metals such as gold and platinum reflect light well and so are shiny. If a mineral is shiny and looks like metal we say it has a metallic lustre. Diamond reflects light even more, and we say it has an adamantine lustre. Minerals that look like glass, such as quartz and tourmaline, have a vitreous lustre. Talc and mica sometimes look like pearls, so we say they have a pearly lustre. Many minerals do not reflect light and so look dull. Kaolinite has a dull lustre.

Types of lustre

Lustre	Appearance
metallic	shiny, metal-like
sub-metallic	uneven, shiny and opaque (not see-through)
adamantine	sparkly
vitreous	shiny, glass-like
greasy	shiny, oily
silky	shimmery like silk
resinous	resin-like
pearly	shimmery like pearls

⬇ Quartz has a vitreous lustre just like a glass you would drink from.

MINERALS UNDER THE MICROSCOPE

Petrological microscope

The microscope used by mineralogists to study minerals is called a petrological microscope.

When **mineralogists** want to find out what types of mineral a rock sample contains they take very thin slices of the rock, called **thin sections**, and examine them under a microscope.

When the rocks are magnified in this way, we can see the individual minerals they contain. Mineralogists can identify minerals under a microscope by looking through a special filter that makes the minerals have bright colours. Scientists can study these minerals and use their knowledge to work out what they are.

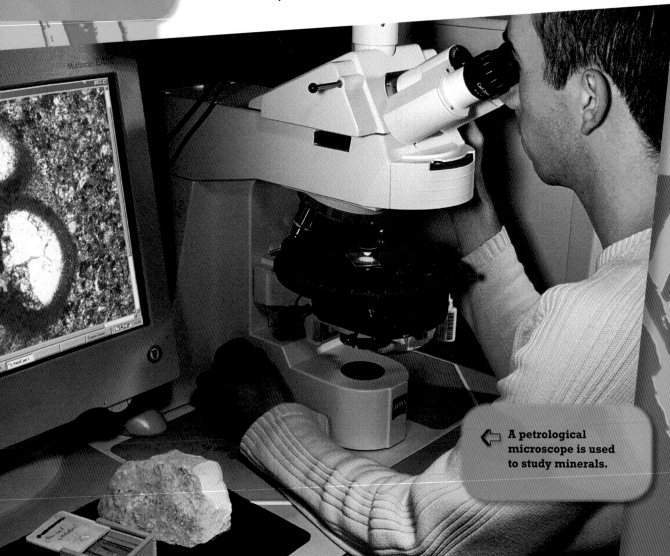

A petrological microscope is used to study minerals.

An electron microscope is a very powerful microscope that can be used to study very small mineral grains that are too small to see under a petrological microscope. A petrological microscope can magnify minerals up to 2,000 times, but the electron microscope can magnify minerals up to 1,000,000 times.

Micrographs

A photograph taken through a microscope is called a **micrograph**. Micrographs show the individual crystals of the minerals in rocks.

If you look at a very thin slice of rock under a petrological microscope the minerals appear brightly coloured.

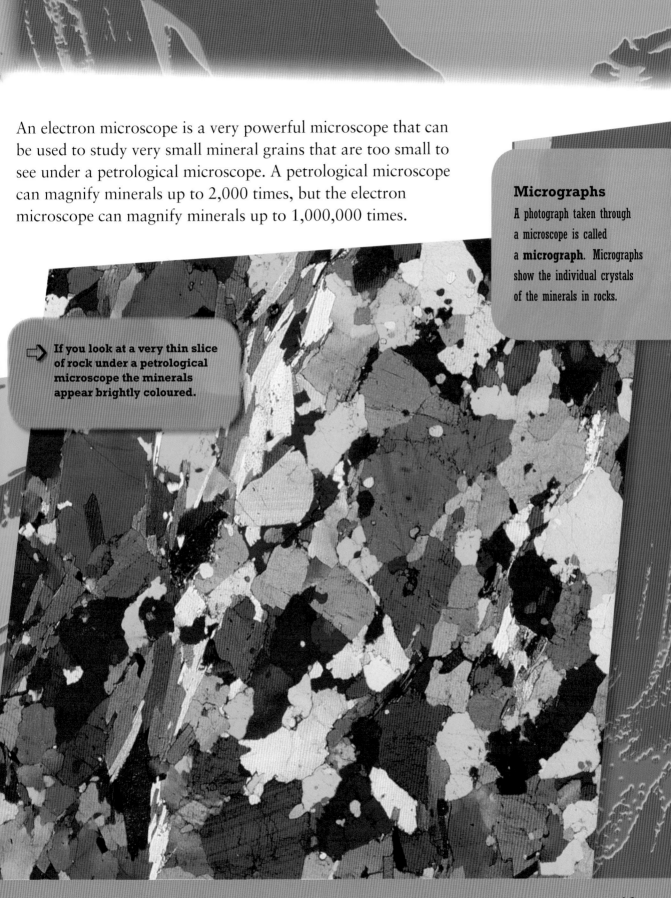

CONCLUSION

Minerals are naturally occurring solid substances that form rocks. The most common minerals on Earth are the silicate minerals, but other important mineral groups include oxides, sulphates, sulphides, halides, carbonates, phosphates, and **native elements**.

Most minerals form deep inside Earth as hot liquid material **crystallizes** into solid minerals. Different combinations of **elements** form different minerals. The rocks of Earth's **crust** are made from about 30 common rock-forming minerals. Rare and beautiful minerals can be found in **mineral veins** and **geodes**.

There are more than 4,000 minerals on Earth so **mineralogists** have a hard time identifying them all. Minerals can be identified according to their colour, **streak**, shape, hardness, **density**, **cleavage**, and **lustre**. Mineralogists can also use special microscopes to help identify minerals.

Humans have used minerals for thousands of years. Minerals have been mined for the metals and **gemstones** they contain, and have been used for many things, from paint to pottery, to jewellery, to electronic devices.

⇨ **Opal means precious stone. It is a type of quartz that looks like coloured glass.**

FIND OUT MORE

Books

1000 Things You Should Know About Rocks and Minerals,
Chris and Helen Pellant (Miles Kelly Publishing, 2006)

Earth's Precious Resources: Minerals, Ian Graham
(Heinemann Library, 2005)

How We Use Materials: Rocks and Stones, Rita Storey
and Holly Wallace (Ashgate Publishing, 2006)

Rocks and Minerals, Caroline Bingham
(Dorling Kindersley, 2004)

Using the Internet

Explore the Internet to find out more about minerals. You
can use a search engine, such as www.yahooligans.com,
and type in keywords such as:

* geodes
* diamonds
* mineral veins

Websites

These websites are useful starting places for finding out more
about geology:

www.bbc.co.uk/education/rocks
www.english-nature.org.uk/geology
www.oum.ox.ac.uk/thezone
www.rocksforkids.com
www.rockwatch.org.uk

GLOSSARY

atom tiny particle that elements and minerals are made from

basalt fine grained igneous rock

classify group together

cleavage how a mineral breaks up

coarse grained large grains

composition what something is made from

compound mixture of elements

core central layer of Earth

crust thin surface layer of Earth

crystal structure within a mineral

crystallization cooling and hardening of magma to form igneous rock

density how heavy something is

deposition laying down weathered rock in a new place

element natural substance made up of atoms

erosion removal and transport of weathered rock

evaporate turn into a gas

extract take out

fine grained tiny grains

fluorescent substance that glows in ultraviolet light

gemstone mineral that is cut and polished for use in jewellery

geode hollow rock lined with crystals

granite hard, igneous rock

igneous rock rock formed from magma either under ground or at Earth's surface

impurity invading substance that enters another substance when it is growing

lattice three-dimensional pattern or framework

lava name for magma when it reaches the surface of Earth

lustre how shiny a metal is

magma molten rock from the mantle

mantle hot layer of Earth beneath the crust

metal ore mixture of minerals that contain useful metals

metamorphic rock rock formed when igneous or sedimentary rocks are changed by heat or pressure

micrograph photograph taken through a microscope

mineralogist scientist who studies minerals

mineral vein sheet of minerals that grows in cracks cutting through rocks

molten melted

native element element that occurs naturally by itself

pigment coloured dye

property characteristic of something

sedimentary rock rock formed from the broken bits of other rocks

smelt heat to a very high temperature

solidify become solid

stalactite thin icicle-shaped lump of rock that forms as water drips from cave ceilings

stalagmite short, stubby column of rock that forms when water drips on to a cave floor and evaporates

streak colour of a mineral when it is powdered

synthetic mineral mineral made artificially

thin section very thin slice of rock mounted on a microscope slide

transparent clear and see-through

weathering breaking down of rock

INDEX